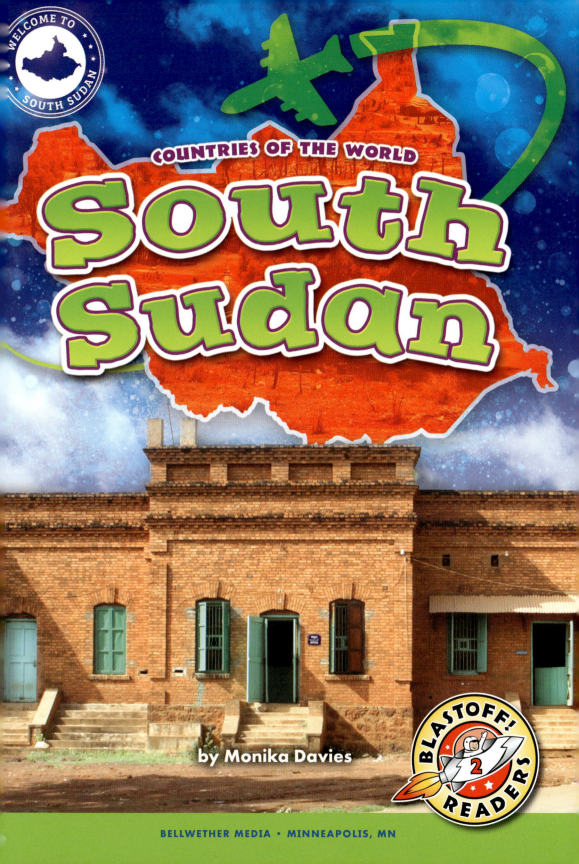

WELCOME TO SOUTH SUDAN

COUNTRIES OF THE WORLD

South Sudan

by Monika Davies

BLASTOFF! READERS 2

BELLWETHER MEDIA • MINNEAPOLIS, MN

Blastoff! Readers are carefully developed by literacy experts to build reading stamina and move students toward fluency by combining standards-based content with developmentally appropriate text.

LEVELS

Level 1 provides the most support through repetition of high-frequency words, light text, predictable sentence patterns, and strong visual support.

Level 2 offers early readers a bit more challenge through varied sentences, increased text load, and text-supportive special features.

Level 3 advances early-fluent readers toward fluency through increased text load, less reliance on photos, advancing concepts, longer sentences, and more complex special features.

★ **Blastoff! Universe**

Reading Level

Grade K

Grades 1–3

Grade 4

This edition first published in 2024 by Bellwether Media, Inc.

No part of this publication may be reproduced in whole or in part without written permission of the publisher. For information regarding permission, write to Bellwether Media, Inc., Attention: Permissions Department, 6012 Blue Circle Drive, Minnetonka, MN 55343.

Library of Congress Cataloging-in-Publication Data

Names: Davies, Monika, author.
Title: South Sudan / by Monika Davies.
Other titles: Blastoff! readers. 2, Countries of the world.
Description: Minneapolis, MN : Bellwether Media, 2024. | Series: Blastoff! Readers. Countries of the world | Includes bibliographical references and index. | Audience: Ages 5-8 | Audience: Grades 2-3 | Summary: "Relevant images match informative text in this introduction to South Sudan. Intended for students in kindergarten through third grade"-- Provided by publisher.
Identifiers: LCCN 2023003568 (print) | LCCN 2023003569 (ebook) | ISBN 9798886874310 (library binding) | ISBN 9798886876192 (ebook)
Subjects: LCSH: South Sudan–Juvenile literature.
Classification: LCC DT159.2 .D38 2024 (print) | LCC DT159.2 (ebook) | DDC 962.905--dc23/eng/20230131
LC record available at https://lccn.loc.gov/2023003568
LC ebook record available at https://lccn.loc.gov/2023003569

Text copyright © 2024 by Bellwether Media, Inc. BLASTOFF! READERS and associated logos are trademarks and/or registered trademarks of Bellwether Media, Inc.

Editor: Rebecca Sabelko   Designer: Gabriel Hilger

Printed in the United States of America, North Mankato, MN.

Table of Contents

All About South Sudan	4
Land and Animals	6
Life in South Sudan	12
South Sudan Facts	20
Glossary	22
To Learn More	23
Index	24

All About South Sudan

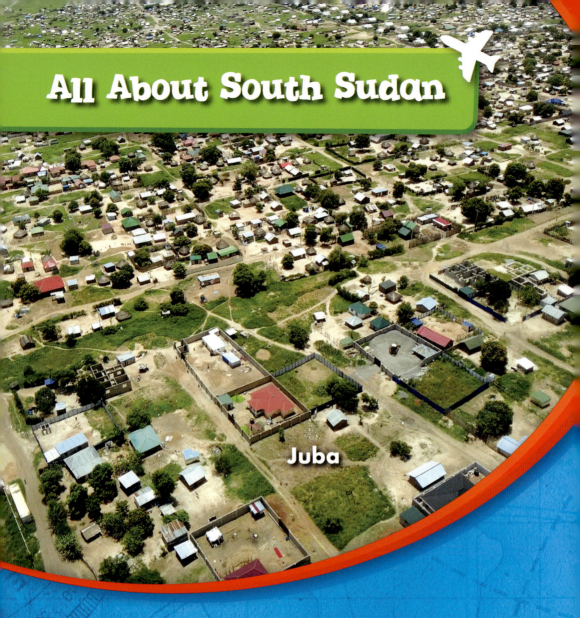

Juba

South Sudan is in eastern Africa. Its capital is Juba.

South Sudan is the world's youngest nation. It became a country in 2011.

Land and Animals

The White Nile River flows through South Sudan. It forms a central **wetland** called the Sudd.

Plateaus rise in the west. Mountains stand tall in the south.

Boya Mountains

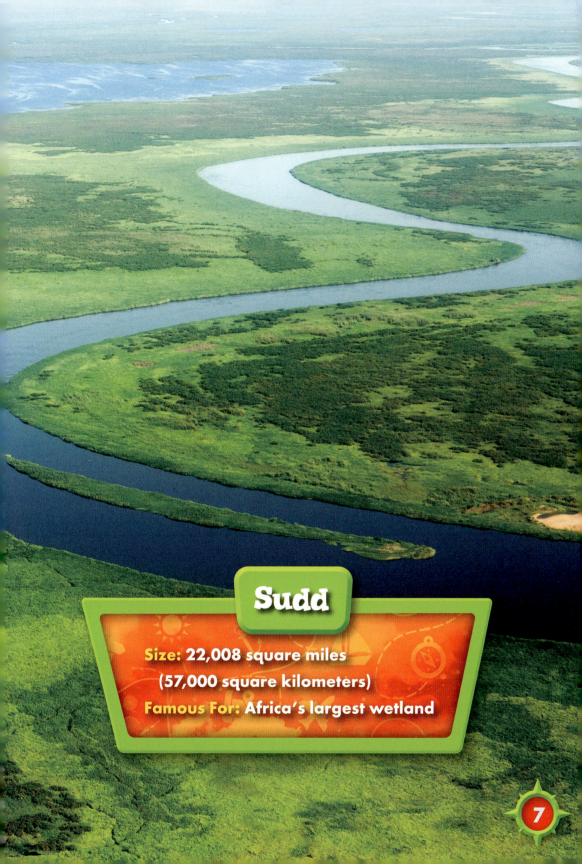

Sudd

Size: 22,008 square miles (57,000 square kilometers)
Famous For: Africa's largest wetland

South Sudan is very hot.
It has a wet and a dry season.

The wet season lasts most of the year. Most areas get around 40 inches (102 centimeters) of rain!

Many animals call South Sudan home. African elephants **wander** the Sudd. Lechwe eat grasses in the wetland.

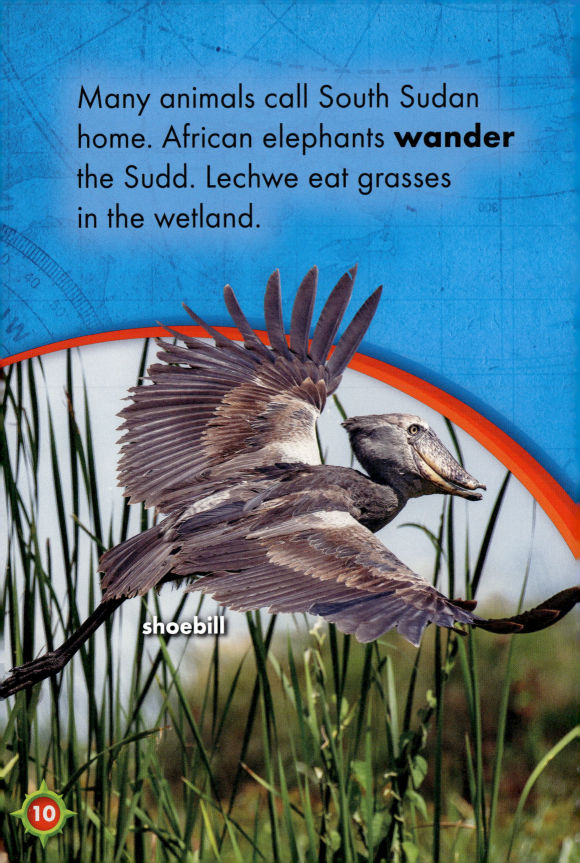

shoebill

Animals of South Sudan

African savanna elephant

Nile lechwe

Nile perch

shoebill

Perch swim in the rivers. Shoebills fly overhead.

Life in South Sudan

Many **ethnic** groups live in South Sudan. Most are **Christians**.

English is the main language. Bari and other languages are spoken, too.

Christian church

basketball

wrestling

Wrestling matches are big events. Many people play basketball or soccer. Some hike in the national parks.

People share **traditions** through storytelling.

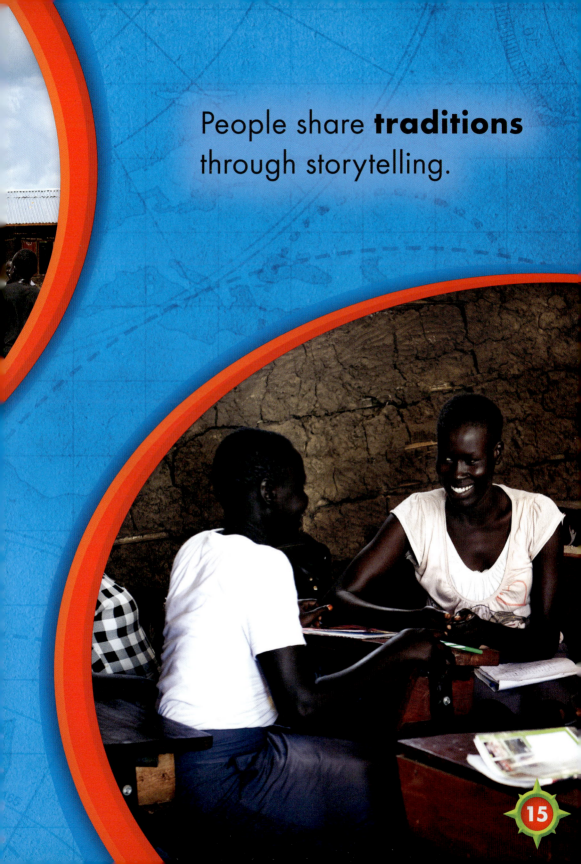

A flatbread called *kisra* is a **staple**. Peanuts are used in many foods.

South Sudanese Foods

kisra

asīda

ful

A porridge called *asīda* is often paired with stews. *Ful* is mashed beans with spices.

Many people **celebrate** Christmas. Families go to church.

Independence Day

Independence Day is on July 9. People go to parades. Holidays bring South Sudan's people together!

South Sudan Facts

Size:
248,777 square miles
(644,329 square kilometers)

Population:
11,544,905 (2022)

National Holiday:
Independence Day (July 9)

Main Languages:
English, Arabic, and ethnic languages including Bari

Capital City:
Juba

Famous Face

Name: Emmanuel Jal

Famous For: author, musician, and activist

Religions

- Muslim: 6%
- other: 1%
- Christian: 60%
- folk religion: 33%

Top Landmarks

Boma National Park

Mount Kinyeti

White Nile River

Glossary

celebrate—to do something special or fun for an event, occasion, or holiday

Christians—people who believe in the words of Jesus Christ

ethnic—related to races or large groups of people who share things such as customs, religion, and language

plateaus—flat, raised areas of land

staple—a widely used food or other item

traditions—the customs, ideas, or beliefs handed down from one generation to the next

wander—to move around without a specific direction

wetland—an area of land that is covered with low levels of water for most of the year

To Learn More

AT THE LIBRARY

Duling, Kaitlyn. *African Elephants*. Minneapolis, Minn.: Bellwether Media, 2020.

Hansen, Grace. *Shoebills*. Minneapolis, Minn.: Abdo Kids Jumbo, 2021.

Wilkins, Veronica B. *Explore Africa*. Minneapolis, Minn.: Jump!, 2020.

ON THE WEB

FACTSURFER

Factsurfer.com gives you a safe, fun way to find more information.

1. Go to www.factsurfer.com.

2. Enter "South Sudan" into the search box and click 🔍.

3. Select your book cover to see a list of related content.

Index

Africa, 4
animals, 10, 11
Bari, 12, 13
basketball, 14
capital (see Juba)
Christians, 12
Christmas, 18
dry season, 8
English, 12, 13
food, 16, 17
hike, 14
Independence Day, 19
Juba, 4, 5
map, 5
mountains, 6
national parks, 14
people, 14, 15, 18, 19
plateaus, 6
rain, 9
river, 6, 11
say hello, 13
soccer, 14
South Sudan facts, 20-21
storytelling, 15
Sudd, 6, 7, 10
wet season, 8, 9
White Nile River, 6
wrestling, 14

The images in this book are reproduced through the courtesy of: Frederique Cifuentes Mørgan/ Alamy, front cover; Svetlanko, front cover, pp. 8-9; Phototreat, pp. 2-3; railway fx, p. 3; John Wollwerth, pp. 4-5; Eric Lafforgue/ Alamy, p. 6; Mike Goldwater/ Alamy, pp. 6-7; robertharding/ Alamy, p. 9; Petr Simon, pp. 10-11; Ludwig Endres, p. 11 (African savanna elephant); Danny Iacob, p. 11 (Nile lechwe); Daiju Azuma/ Wikipedia, p. 11 (Nile perch); Masayuki, p. 11 (shoebill); mtcurado, p. 12; Eric Lafforgue/Art in All of Us / Contributor/ Getty Images, pp. 12-13; Richard Juilliart, pp. 14-15, 15; klublu, p. 14 (wrestling); UDAZKENA/ Alamy, p. 16 (*kisra*); Alexander Mychko, p. 16 (*asida*); Fanfo, p. 16 (*ful*); Spencer Platt / Staff/ Getty Images, p. 17; REUTERS/ Alamy, pp. 18-19; titoOnz, p. 20 (flag); Tore Sætre/ Wikipedia, p. 20 (Emmanuel Jal); Gallo Images/ Alamy, p. 21 (Boma National Park); AlMikhin/ Wikipedia, p. 21 (Mount Kinyeti); John Wollwerth, p. 21 (White Nile River); miroslav chytil, pp. 22-23.